A FIGHT FOR FAITH
A Life in Short

A Fight For Faith
A Life in Short

Terrie L. Knox

Flying Scroll Publishing LLC.

Habakkuk 2:2
And the Lord answered me, and said, Write the vision,
and make it plain upon tables, that he may run that
readeth it.

1st Printing

A Fight For Faith
A Life in Short
ISBN 0-9742432-1-3
Copyright 2003 by:

Flying Scroll Publishing
P.O. Box 246
Fort Atkinson, WI 53538

Cover design: Sy Chung and Sue Callender

To My Father

Who Lost the Battle.

Acknowledgements

Who can I thank but God, for showing me the world through a language that can say so much with so few words?

Who can I thank but God, for giving me all I needed so that I could walk on in Him and see His gifts become a reality in my life?

I also thank Jessica, my daughter, who not only could speak my language but was drawn to it. I thank God for teaching us both how to communicate, giving us both the courage and strength to get to know each other and for maintaining our love so we could work together towards this new beginning.

And I thank all those of the Red Shield whose prayers have kept me going.

PREFACE

Zechariah 5:1
I looked again—and there before me was a flying scroll!
NIV

Habakkuk 2:2
Then the Lord replied: "Write down the revelation and make it plain on tablets so that a herald may run with it. NIV

It took me over ten years, through my relationship with Christ, to sort out my intentions for publishing my books. It all started with a simple need to write. Thus, <u>The Barometric Frog</u>, a humorous murder mystery, flowed from my heart through my fingertips in a slow but steady beat. I didn't realize until I was at the last chapter that it was a metaphor of my life. And until I was able to face the truths I spoke of in the prologue and epilogue, I didn't realize just how much I was trying to carry in my life, how much I was trying to heal on my own in isolation.

As God led me through all I had to face within the safety of metaphor, He gave me my poetry to pick up details that I missed. <u>A Fight For Faith</u> evolved as my second book.

Through it all, I held onto my relationship with Christ knowing that He was my only hope. My prayer life unfolded and I was strengthened through the scriptures. I was able to find meaning in words that before always sent me into vicious whirlwinds of emotional debate. Thus, <u>Worrisome Words</u> soon became the third book. A trilogy had been established...my life in metaphor and poetry and the understanding that came from surviving it.

Once I started writing, I could not stop. God gave me an avenue to continue my writing as the editor of a monthly newsletter, The Red Shield. The Red Shield Ministries is a ministry of intercession, which reaches out to the whole body of Christ. Many on our mailing list are prisoners. As I worked more and more with prisoners and those isolated by other situations, I found myself crying out for justice with a passion I hadn't known for years. But then I began to wonder if justice was possible. I wondered if anyone, including myself, knew what justice was.

Corresponding and visiting with prisoners and others isolated from society opened my eyes to many of the wrongs, which are done in the name of justice. The move to clean up our streets by locking up the bad guys has led to overcrowded prisons and more injustices. The damage done to children and relationships due to addictions and crime seemed overwhelming. My reminders to forgive and submit to authority were lost in the absurdity of the situations. And I was left once again feeling hopeless within this stagnant mire. Prison time and isolation is a consequence of chosen actions. But this time doesn't relieve the debt of the offense or change the person; it only separates those who need help most.

As we look at all the pain and injustices in our lives and the lives of others, we choose to face them with or without forgiveness. If we choose not to forgive, we must pick a price with which the debt can be paid. An eye for an eye is often the only example we have ever seen. But money or like-pain cannot restore the lives that were injured. Healing doesn't come from canceled debt. Thus our lives are still not whole, not restored and justice can never be found. We find ourselves locked in a never ending cycle of revenge and fear. It is then when the term victim takes on a new meaning, one of hopeless condemnation.

I found that forgiveness is our only hope. And healing is our only chance of restoration. Forgiveness doesn't mean to forget. Even Jesus wrote about the sins that were committed against Him. The Bible discloses the wrong that was done to Him... but it also contains the promises that He gives to those who believe in Him. In love, God speaks the truth. And in love, God leads us through the pain of that truth into the healing that He promises.

As I move ahead to publish these books and start the Flying Scroll Publishing company, I again have to ask why. Revealing the pain that was in my life is certainly not going to take it away. And starting a publishing company in this glutted, failing environment with the resulting profits would not be a wise investment according to any worldly perspective. So why continue? There is but one reason and that is my need to example that which God has given me in this process.

Ephesians 5:8-10
For ye were sometimes darkness, but now are ye light in the Lord: walk as children of light: (For the fruit of the Spirit is in all goodness and righteousness and truth;) Proving what is acceptable unto the Lord. KJV

By publishing my books I am walking in God's word by living in the light of exposure and moving beyond any required payment of debt. I have chosen to forgive, to cancel any debt owed me, and am seeking an authority above any on this earth. I am seeking God's healing and justice. By starting the Flying Scroll Publishing company, I am trusting God's promise to restore me and to open the doors for this opportunity of new beginnings for others who choose His way.

Psalm 60:4
Thou hast given a banner to them that fear thee, that it may be displayed because of the truth. Selah. KJV

Terrie L. Knox

November 7, 2002

FORWARD

There are times when we believe that our lives are not yielding what is desired. But what we might consider a dry spell might well be a metamorphosis, like a larvae growing into the adult stage of a beautiful butterfly. Perhaps what is occurring is our transformation during the pupa stage...dry spell...transformation...metamorphosis.

Are we dissolving as sugar does in water having no form? Or are we being transformed by the pattern of the Divine?

Deuteronomy 6:10
And it shall be, when the Lord thy God shall have brought thee into the land which he sware unto thy fathers, to Abraham, to Isaac, and to Jacob, to give thee great and goodly cities, which thou buildedst not.

God brings healing to damaged emotions by countless methods. A vision of a brighter today starts with the journey of exposing one's damaged emotions to God's soothing balm.

II Corinthians 3:18
But we all, with open face beholding as in a glass the glory of the Lord, are changed into the same image from glory to glory, even as by the Spirit of the Lord.
KJV

I believe that the <u>Barometric Frog, A Fight For Faith,</u> and <u>Worrisome Words</u> were written so the wonderful healing of God would be visible to all who might profit from it.

These books need to be placed not only in the

hands of the victims of sexual abuse but the abuser's hands and the community's. They are not a books of self pity nor condemnation. However, they are channels through which emotional healing is conveyed. We stop succumbing to damaged emotions because we are more than conquerors!

I am deeply moved by Knox's sincerity and willingness to share her own life in metaphor, poetry and essay. Direction and encouragement for emotional healing are offered by her efforts within the pages of these books. Call them, if you will, the essence of emotional healing.

There is prosperity within the cocoon. The character development that results is a beautiful creature beyond description. Rest in the Lord and wait patiently for Him. (Psalm 37:7)

Raul V. Garza

May 2003

Introduction

Early in May of 1990, my mother received a call from an old friend who heard a rumor that my father was dead. Not knowing what to do, my mother turned to me. I contacted the mortician in search of the truth. He was horrified at having to tell me of my father's demise but I was given the information I needed. My father had driven out of town, walked to the side of the road, pointed his shotgun to his face and pulled the trigger. My brothers were dealing with it as well as they could. They had tried to carry out my father's last wish... that I (as well as my mother and my two sisters) would not be at his funeral. Thus they did not inform us of his death.

I have chosen to forgive my father and my brothers. I also prayed that God would remind me of something that I could remember my father for that would move me beyond the pain of his wasted life. Since then, God has given me hope that my father is with Him in heaven. And after all these years, God reminded me of the wooden doll case that my father made for me one Christmas. I could see his hard and callused hands cutting and sanding the wood and fitting the clothes rack and drawer into place. This was something very frivolous and unnecessary. It was meant for fun and pleasure... not survival.

With this vision came a feeling of intense love lost in a furnace burning white hot with hatred, anger and frustration. It was a furnace that my father so desperately tried to cool with the alcohol that destroyed his life. With this vision I was able to see through that blazing flame into the depths of his core, that core of a father's love...and its failure.

Our choice is our most powerful weapon to lead us into the victory that is ours through Christ. It is the first thing that we, in our human limitations, try to take from others in an attempt to push them or ourselves to our own version of success. But it is also the only thing that can keep us from becoming victims of the choices of others.

I chose to forgive, but I also choose to stand behind the truth. It is a choice that has taken more determination than I had. But through Christ all things are possible. And it is in facing the truth that we are set free.

Terrie L. Knox

May 22, 2001

A FIGHT FOR FAITH
A Life in Short

TO THE TIRED

Heavy heavens pressure the heart,
To dreams sheltered from the sky.
But as with clouds these dreams conclude
In reflections of rays or drenched lies.

So each day I pray for the sense
To ruffle my feathers when in stress.
So that I might quickly recover
And soar through the bright expanse.

CUSTODY

The silence of decision breaks
As the judge clears his throat.
The mirage of security disintegrates
When a man emerges from the robe.

Bloodshot eyes magnified by lenses,
Impatience etched between untidy brows,
Hands scrubbed clean leave no traces
Of the future they despotically hold.

Each detail further decomposes
The purple illusion trusted by all.
The life that his denuded grasp dangles,
Struggles helplessly in the panic of the fall.

Fear lives beyond hallucination,
When a man donning the robe of sanctity
Decides against a commendation,
Denouncing a slight entity.

YOUNG LOGIC

You and me hafta talk.
Right Mom?

      Sure, what about?

Horses, kitty cats, and cows.

      OK.

I like to ride cows
    and then I put on a cowboy hat
and ride and ride.

      ...Ah, it's horses you ride.

Oh yeah, and giddy-up.
We can talk about birthdays too.

      What about birthdays?

I have birthdays,
   and cards,
  cause I'm three.

      That's right.

Why is my daddy in Virginia?

      Because that's where he lives.

He gave me a card and presents. Was he here?

> No, he sent them through the mail.
> And it comes on an airplane.

Birds can fly.

> Yes.

I can't fly. I don't have feathers.

Mom, let's talk about cards. What does this one say?

> Have a Happy Birthday. Love Daddy
> and Missy.

Who's Missy.

> Your father's wife.

Oh yeah... But then who are you?

> I'm your mother.

Oh yeah. I love you Mom.

COLLEGE

To the campus she came at last
To sow fields she needed.
But the garden she planned to reap
Kept needin' more seedin'.

When some seeds sprouted
She forgot her past woe.
She was ready to rejoice till
She had to man the hoe.

But hard she did work
For she knew she was needin'.
The way to a good harvest
Is to keep on weedin'.

At last her acres ripen'd
And a pickin' she went,
Smilen' cause the crops she grew
Would pay for the seeds spent.

But the full basket she peddled
Was not quite the right goal.
For some it was too expensive,
Others griped 'bout the hole.

HALLOWEEN

A turbulent tummy

in a bed

of

empty

wrappers.

ASTARTE

Crickets so loud at night
when all is covered, a selective ear,
Easily forgotten when the simple security of
a life surviving
accepts the strife of the eye.
Inherents who resume their place only when
the silence
of solitude returns.
...Astarte.

THANKSGIVING

When all
are allowed
to
gobble.

THE CHITINOUS FUGUE

My mind wanders through the catacombs of
life
Resting on the fragments of the meaningless
few
As half a shell sits with empty pride
On a shelf next to Nemo.
So are the stools slightly laden
With pieces of years accumulating
Till all that is seen, a vapid asylum,
Lost in the tides of the tombs.

FAIRY TALES

If the sun were always shining,
Would the princess be alive?
Would she be laughing and singing,
With an eternal sparkle in her eye?

If the moon reigned forever,
Would the kingdom seduce the stars?
Would the ecstasy and comfort continue
While wrapped in her lover's arms?

If the past had never been,
Would fairy tales be true?
Would the princess be alive,
So she could believe in you?

DIDYMIUM

Cached cans
Under a daffodil daze.
Wilhelm's eyes in every gaze.
Disney music from Harlem's maze.
A rainbow of color from the prisms of gray.

CHRISTMAS EVE

Trying to

ignore

the clock's

slow

tick.

DON

Look around you

To find

The filth in the corners of cavernous minds.

Open your eyes.

Naive,

To think the Damsks could actually see.

Tell the children to beware.

Symbiosis is a quixotic's lair.

But to efface the terrene

One must

Believe in more than an incubus.

IN DEFENSE OF THE VIRUS

Most say the virus is not life
But pre-stages of its true essence.
Though without the vitalistic strife
Who'd be in charge of its subsistence?

Perhaps tis just a parasite,
One far beyond its time,
Perfecting the sporozoa's fight
To withstand the outside clime.

For in its sad dependent plight
To get to new addresses,
It made its belt extremely tight
And carries just recesses.

This lack of excess baggage
Makes metabolism a test.
But then it takes the right cell hostage.
Now is it host or guest?

If tis an evolved transposon,
From those in the higher branches,
Then a lofty place in the tree is won.
Remember... evolution ner' regresses.

SPRING IRONY

The fresh smell
of rain
Through dust covered
screens.

A MOURNFUL EYE

Weddings in white
Only pristine traditions,
Not geared to a world with such complications.
To dance, it takes one.
No need to bother;
Victorian morals are no longer.
Titles once thought
Respect not insult,
Only intimate greetings are the result.
"I don't approve."
Is the same old reply,
But now comes from experience's mournful
eye.

RIVER REFLECTIONS

The lights of civilization
look best
at night across the river.
Late fall, before ice
Yet after the bite of frost
When detoured boatmen
do not
Erupt quiet waters
to reflect
the zillion dirty details.

INTERRUPTED VIEW

The night lay softly on the snow.
The moon makes crooked limbs multiply
within sight.
The waves silently crash against rocks
rugged and invincible,
lining the cold towers.
Ships of ice patrol, too close, become more.
A lone owl circles low to make a surviving dive.
Life below shudders to its last step.
Majestic growth swells all eyes
Alone they see the world they stage.
Then inner light floods concave angles
Till owls disappear into flawed crystals.

LATE SPRING

Over-fluffed robins

Wistfully wait

For the worms to warm up.

THE NEW IMMIGRANT

Wars fought,
dowries gambled,
ships sailed.
Memories not mine.
Enough to but tease
The need.

One by one they disappear,
Minds that hold such trivia.
Smooth stones give no clues
from whence they came,
gone.
Only shadows where they went.

Yet time, insatiably persistent,
A ceaseless activist.
Defining durability,
a generation's demise.
Betraying Berlitz
and me.

ANTS IN AMBER

Life locked in life
A folded antenna
Bubbled and bent and clouded in resin.

Truth in details
All within reach.
Life's very meaning in a nucleic leash.

A folded antenna...
Or broken with care?
The most patient virus lays his lair.

Life locked in life
No keys allowed.
Destroy the vessel to clear the cloud.

My past and my present
All there to ponder,
Like a polished pendant of ants in amber.

SINS OF OUR FATHERS

The blessed babe arrived today
Reaching for security.
But bruised and battered there she lay
And in survival walked away
From all in need.

Through whose eyes now, Lord?
Through whose eyes now?
When rosy lenses crumble
Over thorny crowns we stumble.
Through whose eyes now?

Great protector here am I.
The world is worth but a sigh.
I'll hide your eyes so do not try
To understand the ways gone by
Of those in need.

Through whose eyes now, Lord?
Through whose eyes now?
When rosy lenses crumble
Over thorny crowns we stumble.
Through whose eyes now?

The gavel slams on oaken top.
Don't ask why you have to stop.
To see the light you follow rules
And give them out to all the fools.
To those who need.

Through whose eyes now, Lord?
Through whose eyes now?
When rosy lenses crumble
Over thorny crowns we stumble.
Through whose eyes now?

You are The Way, Lord.
I've tried You well.
Step by step my life does tell
The why and way of life with You.
For all do need.

Through Your eyes now, Lord.
Through Your eyes now.
Help me survive as You see best
With all the glory of the test
Through Your eyes now.

Books by Terrie L. Knox

The Barometric Frog
$13.95

A Fight For Faith
A Life in Short
$8.00

Worrisome Words
A Spiritual Study
$10.95

NOT FOR RESALE!
John 12:24, 26
I tell you the truth, unless a kernel of wheat falls to the ground and dies, it remains only a single seed. But if it dies, it produces many seeds.
Whoever serves me must follow me; and where I am, my servant also will be. My Father will honor the one who serves me. NIV

The Red Shield is a ministry of worldwide intercession that reaches out to the whole body of Christ, helping them to mature and focus on God's will in their lives.

**For Further Information on
The Red Shield Ministries**

**Send inquiries and/or
Prayer Requests
To:**

**Red Shield Ministries
P.O. Box 81
Fort Atkinson, WI 53538**